curious?about

AREA 51

BY GILLIA M. OLSON

AMICUS LEARNING

What are you

curious about?

Curious About is published by
Amicus Learning, an imprint of Amicus
P.O. Box 227
Mankato, MN 56002
www.amicuspublishing.us

Editor: Ana Brauer
Series Designer: Kathleen Petelinsek
Book Designer and Photo Researcher: Emily Dietz

Library of Congress Cataloging-in-Publication Data
Names: Olson, Gillia M., author. | Olson, Gillia M. Curious about unexplained mysteries.
Title: Curious about Area 51 / by Gillia M. Olson.
Description: Mankato, MN : Amicus Learning, [2025] | Series: Curious about unexplained mysteries | Includes bibliographical references and index. | Audience: Ages 6–9 | Audience: Grades 2–3 | Summary: "What really happens at Area 51? Learn about this unexplained mystery in this question-and-answer book for elementary-aged readers. Includes infographics, table of contents, glossary, books and websites for further research, and index"— Provided by publisher.
Identifiers: LCCN 2024014737 (print) | LCCN 2024014738 (ebook) | ISBN 9798892000918 (library binding) | ISBN 9798892001496 (paperback) | ISBN 9798892002073 (ebook)
Subjects: LCSH: Conspiracy theories—Nevada—Area 51—Juvenile literature. | Area 51 (Nev.)—Juvenile literature.
Classification: LCC UG634.5.A74 O47 2025 (print) | LCC UG634.5.A74 (ebook) | DDC 358.4170979314—dc23/eng/20240402
LC record available at https://lccn.loc.gov/2024014737
LC ebook record available at https://lccn.loc.gov/2024014738

Photo Credits: Alamy Stock Photo/Tibbut Archive, 9 (*middle*); Getty Images/BRIDGET BENNETT, 7, DigitalGlobe ScapeWare3d, 4–5, Keystone, 9 (*second from top*), Photo 12, 9 (*top*); NASA, 16–17; Noun Project/Adrien Coquet, 22, 23, Esteban Sandoval, 7, 22, 23; rationalwiki/Unknown, 12–13; Shutterstock/andrea crisante, cover, 1, BrianPIrwin, 19, chrupka, 6, Fer Gregory, 2, 15, JohnWR, 3, 20–21, ktsdesign, 10–11, Steve Lagreca, 14, ZAB Photographie, cover, 1; Wikimedia Commons/Juergen Schiffmann, 9 (*bottom*), U.S. Air Force photo by Master Sgt. Rose Reynolds, 2, 8, ZLEA, 9 (*second from bottom*)

Printed in China

CHAPTER ONE

Is Area 51 real?

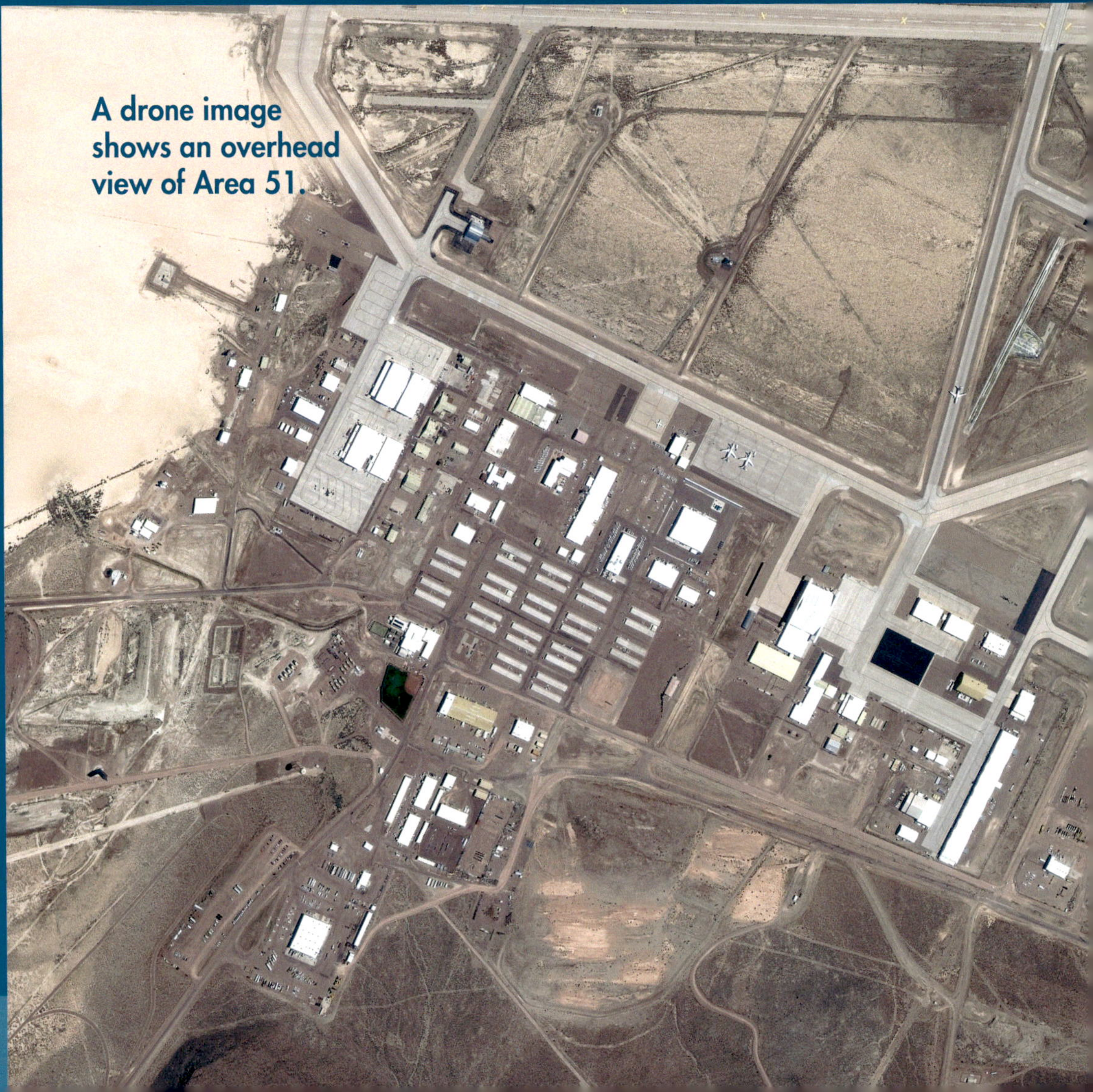

A drone image shows an overhead view of Area 51.

Yes, Area 51 is real. It's a United States **military base**. The government studies and makes planes there. The base is famous for stories about alien spaceships. Has it ever held an **unidentified** flying object, or a UFO? That is another question.

DID YOU KNOW?
Area 51 was created in 1955. The government did not admit it was there until 2013.

Where is it?

Area 51 is in southern Nevada. It's in the middle of a desert. It's part of the Nevada Test and Training Range. The base's secrets are well protected. People who don't work there can't get near it.

Signs around the base warn people to stay away.

OTHER NAMES FOR AREA 51

- Homey Airport
- Paradise Ranch
- The Box
- Dreamland
- Groom Lake

Why was it created?

Spy planes like the U-2 *Dragon Lady* were built at Area 51.

In the 1950s, the government wanted to make new planes to spy on other countries. The desert was the perfect spot for a secret base. No one lived nearby. The U-2 spy plane was made in Area 51.

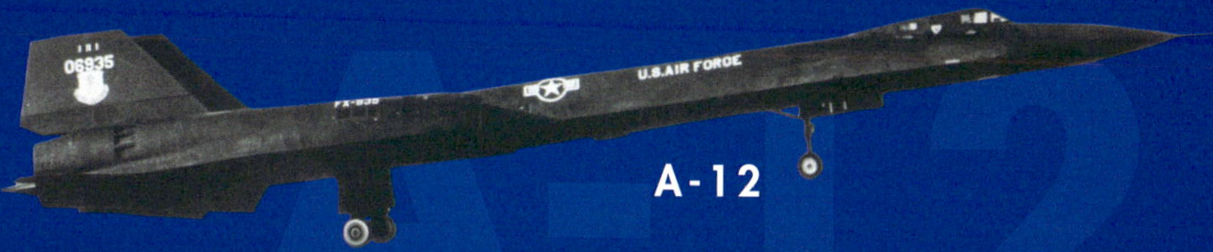

A-12

SR-71 BLACKBIRD

TACIT BLUE

DRONES

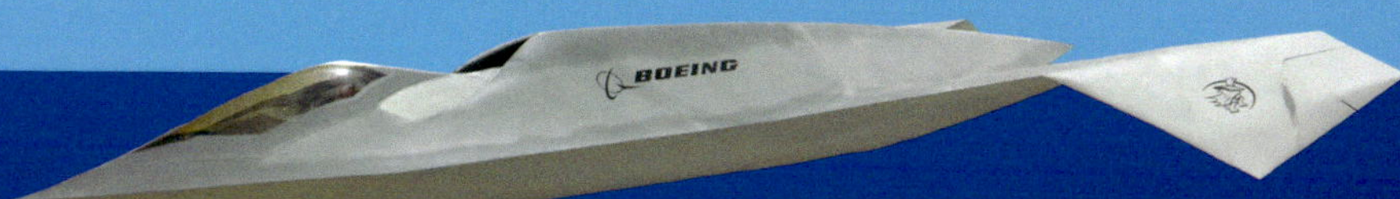

BIRD OF PREY

CHAPTER TWO

When did UFO stories start?

Any unknown object in the sky could be a UFO.

Strange sightings began soon after the base opened. In 1959, some people said they saw a bright green object in the sky. The object moved faster than any known plane. People probably saw test flights of the new aircraft made at Area 51.

No one knows for sure if Robert Lazar ever actually worked at Area 51.

What about alien spaceships?

In 1989, Robert Lazar said he worked at Area 51. He said he studied alien aircraft to find out how it worked. Officials deny he ever worked there. Scientists did study planes at Area 51. But the planes were just from other countries.

Where else do UFO stories happen?

The secret base has been linked to other famous stories. In 1947, something crashed in Roswell, New Mexico. Military people collected the craft. Later, local people said it was a UFO. There is no **proof** that it was an alien ship.

After Roswell, people started to look for proof of flying saucers.

What else is linked to Area 51?

DID YOU KNOW?
Astronauts did train at the Nevada Test Site. The desert prepared them for working on the Moon's surface.

The secret base gets pulled into **conspiracy** theories. One theory is that the Moon landing never happened. Some people say the pictures and videos were done in the desert at Area 51 instead. There is no proof. But that doesn't stop people from repeating the story.

The first Moon landing happened in July 1969.

CHAPTER THREE

What happens at Area 51 today?

Area 51 is an active base. The Air Force says it is a training facility. New technology is likely tested there. Its work is not open to the public. Workers are not allowed to talk about it.

Going into Area 51 is not allowed. People who break these rules can go to jail.

Why do people try to go there?

DID YOU KNOW?

Nearly 7 in 10 people think the government knows more about UFOs than it is telling.

Work at the base is still secret. People come from all over the country to see if they can find signs of alien life. Until people know for sure what happens at Area 51, they will be curious about it.

Nearby towns have diners and shops with alien themes.

ASK MORE QUESTIONS

How do people stop conspiracy theories?

What new technology could come from Area 51 in the future?

Try a BIG QUESTION: If alien spacecraft was really found at Area 51, how would that change the world?

SEARCH FOR ANSWERS

Search the library catalog or the Internet.
A librarian, teacher, or parent can help you.

Using Keywords
Find the looking glass.

Keywords are the most important words in your question.

If you want to know about:

- how to debunk conspiracy theories, type: DEBUNKING CONSPIRACIES
- new plane technology, type: NEW AERIAL TECHNOLOGY

LEARN MORE

FIND GOOD SOURCES

Here are some good, safe sources you can use in your research.
Your librarian can help you find more.

Books

Area 51 by Marysa Storm, 2022.

Area 51 by Kenny Abdo, 2020.

Internet Sites

TED-Ed: Why Can't We See Evidence of Alien Life?
https://ed.ted.com/lessons/why-can-t-we-see-evidence-of-alien-life
TED-Ed is a non-profit educational site with videos on many topics.

Wonderopolis: What is Area 51?
https://wonderopolis.org/wonder/what-is-area-51
Wonderopolis is a non-profit site for students and their families.

Every effort has been made to ensure that these websites are appropriate for children. However, because of the nature of the Internet, it is impossible to guarantee that these sites will remain active indefinitely or that their contents will not be altered.

SHARE AND TAKE ACTION

Learn more about space.
Visit a local planetarium or observatory.

Learn more about a career in the Air Force.
Maybe you could work at Area 51 one day!

Attend an air show.
See what amazing things planes can do.

GLOSSARY

conspiracy An idea that explains an event as the result of a secret plot, usually by powerful people or governments.

military base A permanent space occupied by the armed forces.

proof Facts or evidence that show something is true.

unidentified Unknown.

INDEX

About the Author

Gillia Olson is a skeptic by nature but loves all things paranormal. She stays curious and open-minded and hopes you will, too. She lives in southern Minnesota.